This book is dedicated to the thousands of children I have encountered and who have each blessed my life in so many ways.

Published by

Way Opens Press

72 War Trophy Lane
Media, Pennsylvania 19063

Editorial and design services provided by
Rich Schiffer

ISBN 978-0-9981315-1-1

Copyright © 2018 by Way Opens Press
All Rights Reserved
Poem, First Flight, Copyright © 1990 by Rich Schiffer,
used with permission
Printed in the United States of America
October 2018

Second Edition

Soul Returns to Preschool

We make many decisions every day – consciously or unconsciously –
about ourselves and where we hold ourselves as we work with children.

The words in this book are not the words to say to a child, but to yourself.
They are words that create a tender place to hold in your heart
as you work with the child.

Soul Returns to Preschool

A Children's Book for Adults

Art and Text by Jennifer Elam, Ph.D

Prelude

A FEW YEARS AGO, on a beautiful Kentucky spring day, I went for a walk with a little girl who was three. Her name was Amy. As we walked through the woods together, she ran up to a wildflower. Showing me small details inside the flower, Amy said, "Look, Jenny, look at that!" Then she found a rock. "Oh, Jenny, look at this!" It looked like an ordinary rock to me, but she reveled in its shape and coloring. Then she ran and pointed to a beautifully detailed piece of tree bark. With a tone of hushed awe and wonder, she looked straight into my eyes and whispered, "Oh, Jenny!"

That walk was one of the greatest gifts anyone has given me. It taught me to stand in awe of Creation. It taught me to let nature provide me with daily sustenance. Because of that walk with a three-year-old girl, my first utterance of the day is now thanks for the trees outside my window and for the birds that awaken me with their singing. And because of that walk with a three-year-old girl, I now often take walks along a nearby creek.

For eight days in a row one fall, I communed with a pair of blue herons. One day, after missing them for a few weeks, I felt drawn to a part of the creek along which I don't usually walk, and there my heart leapt. Standing stately and still, its gray-blue feathers blending into the trunk of a tree, was one of the herons. I felt blessed to be in the presence of such style and gracefulness.

Sometimes I sit quietly on a rock by the creek. I feel the water rush by. Cares seem to float away as worries find their proper place. My energy rises. Squirrels play and fuss, rustling the leaves. My heart soars. In the water, I see the deep reflection of majestic trees—and realize that Life is all around me. As my own creative spirit begins to flow, I am thankful for Life and Creation.

I thank Amy – and all the other children in my life – for the many lessons they have taught me.

I thank Rich Schiffer, and Helen for all they have taught me about children!

Making Friends – For Eric

At six, you are quicksilver, darting
ahead. But here, having tramped
through our neighbor's wet pasture
to see his young calves, clumped close
to their mothers, you crouch
and take time making friends.

They are curious, blinking
long lashes and licking their lips.
Their damp noses snuffle for scent.
Their legs trot in closer, then
brains catch up, jerk them back
stiffening, raising their tails.

You hunker down there in the mud
and talk to them softly, admiring
the brown one's white spots
either side of her throat, asking
if a dark streak down the black
and white's cheek is a tear.

Was it hours with your daddy
spent fishing that schooled you
to patience like this when you itched
to be at things right off? Or
maybe a gift from your mother,
so early a tamer of gulls?

Or do you just know for yourself
what it means to be scared, to be
eager? To venture, shrink back?
You focus the whole of your longing
on welcome, and wait. Already
so steady, so tenderly wise.
--Helen

First Flight

The child sitting next to me
has such a pretty smile.
Her wandering gaze
settles for a moment
on an unknown
spot in space.
I can sense the wonderment.
I can feel her joy.
For I too
was once a child
on my first flight.

--Rich Schiffer

Foreward

I am so grateful for those young psychologists and others, especially educators, who are excited about working with young children. I am grateful for the 30+ years I was given to work as a psychologist, the last 13 of which were with 3-5-year olds. That is a very special place to be. In Early Intervention, when we play our cards right, we can prevent problems down the road. That is the goal. And how best to get there?

I am very grateful for the amazing training I received as an intern for my Ph.D. at the University of North Carolina – Chapel Hill. The researchers and practitioners at the Frank Porter Graham Child Development Center really got it about how very young children need to be taught differently from older children. There was a compassion in their work that I have seldom seen in schools. Perhaps that came partly from a director whose own child was in Early Intervention, a personal stake in it.

A personal stake in it is often what is needed to provide excellence in service. A personal stake in it, however, often comes into conflict with the perceived "objectivity", that psychologists and other professionals are taught is the mainstay and main evidence of "professionalism." I take issue with that. I believe with all my heart that along with "objectivity", a personal stake in it is critical for true, long-term impact and success with younger children (people of all ages, truth be told).

Children are begging to be seen and heard beyond their (mis)behaviors. Many are hurting and can't please the adults around them. Many have already been expelled from school by age 4. My heart aches and soars while watching these 3-5-year olds. To ground my own work in a broader place of heart and spirit, for one year, when I did an evaluation or a consultation, I also created a poem or painting, as I sent good thoughts, hopes, and wishes to that child. This little book contains excerpts from that year of poems and paintings, excerpts from their hurts I have witnessed and the lights I have seen. Our souls need to be seen and heard! This book is dedicated to the children!

Recently, I heard an interview with a farmer in New Jersey. She was asked what the most important and unique quality a person must have to be a farmer. Her answer was poignant. She said a person must be able to tolerate discomfort. The animals have to be fed and the fields have to be tended whether it is 110°F or minus 30°F. Discomfort is possible. My father was a farmer. One of his quotes I heard repeated at his funeral was, "What does comfort have to do with living real life?" I believe that it is not only farmers that have to be able to tolerate discomfort. Educators have a different version of 110° or minus 30° temperatures. Expecting to always be comfortable is going to set one up for great disappointment.

Introduction

This Children's Book for Adults (especially families and adults working with young children) seeks to integrate the various lives I have lived before my recent retirement as a psychologist. I live what Parker Palmer, well known author and educator, calls a "divided life." I have led a strong and fulfilling academic life as a psychologist, with the last years of practice in Early Intervention. That is a special place to be and I treasure those years. In addition, I have studied spirituality intensely for myself while living at Pendle Hill, a Quaker center for study and contemplation, then was involved in research related to both adult and children's spirituality for 14 years and continue the study informally.

I have also had a travel bug most of my life and love studying different cultures. I had thought of doing my dissertation on cross-cultural practices in special education but found the language barriers difficult for completing a dissertation. Nonetheless, I have visited many school programs in many countries.

In addition, I have studied and practiced creativity/arts and spirituality, leading many workshops, classes, and retreats since 1996 and continue that practice. Creative practices use art to create a balance in left and right brain learning. For too long, our professional work has been weighted toward left-brain activity. I believe that by incorporating the arts, adults can learn as children naturally do, a more left- and right-brained balanced learning.

This work of attempting to integrate many paradigms is messy; many would not tolerate the chaos it brings to one's thinking. There is no "Integrated Life Manual 101." The greater wholeness the integration brings, even if messy, for me has been so worth the effort. The effort brings a richness in awareness that goes beyond the traditional school psychologist's life of focus on the intellect.

My life has truly been a "divided life." I have struggled with the conflicts created by the core parts of my life dictating different values. Soul Returns to Preschool is an integration of that study, research, teaching, and practice in different arenas: an integration of those divided lives.

Recently, while riding down the road, I heard a discussion on the radio about people living unconventional lives. What the speaker said stayed with me. He said that when someone presents ideas that are different, they are viewed either as great (trailblazing), or not. I want to readily admit up front that my life has not been typical, so the integration of the parts of it may work as inspiration for you or it may not.

My hope is that we remain open to sharing the possibilities of heart and soul amidst academic rigor.

Academic Life

As a teacher of human services, then of school psychology in 1980s and 1990s, I found myself drawn to teaching developmental psychology. Until then, my training and practice had been strongly focused in behavioral psychology and I still consider that an important piece of psychology to inform one's practice with children. But there are also many other important parts of each of us that affect our behavior and our functioning in the world. I was so excited when psychologists and educators discovered that social and emotional functioning are important parts of humans, even children. But, my exploration continued.

At the University of North Carolina – Chapel Hill, concurrently with a class on traditional family therapy, I was trained to use a strength-based model of assessment and intervention with children and families in Early Intervention with Dr. Pam Winton. I found this model quite compatible with my need to see children as people first. Psychological protocols focusing on the intellect are necessary but must be in balance with other parts of our lives. This book models the view taken of children with strength-based and compassionate foundational principles as primary. I readily acknowledge the place for objectivity yet see being humans together first as essential. Objectivity must take its rightful place, allowing children and families to be seen as people first.

Diagnosis of pathology is a bona fides role of the psychologist, but there is also a need to balance this with strength and resilience-building for young children and their families. The internalized shame and helplessness I have often seen brought on by diagnostic labeling has no place in our work and must be counter-acted with compassion and affirmations of strength along with skill-building. A strength-based model of psychological practice with young children became very important to me.

As a school psychologist, I work toward helping individuals primarily, with only minor attention to making the institution of education better. As a sociologist, the focus is primarily on institutions and culture. All of these are important.

A strength-based model is consistent with my work as a sociologist in the area of criminology. The concept of the school-to-prison pipeline is very real. Strength-based practices could be employed to interrupt that cycle.

See Appendix I for more about strength-based practices (so important this deserves a book of its own).

Study of the Spiritual Life and Children's Spirituality Research

Grown men may learn from very little children, for the hearts of little children are pure, and therefore, the Great Spirit may show to them many things which older people miss.
—Black Elk, Ogala Lakota Medicine Man, 1863-1950

While in graduate school, I became aware of Quakers. I found them to appreciate stillness, social justice, and many more of the things that I value. In 1995, at the suggestion of an educator, Parker Palmer, I went to Pendle Hill. As I said, Parker writes about a life I was leading as a "divided life."

Mine was very divided: divided by place (KY and PA) and by values in my profession. Core parts of my spiritual life and professional life were not on the same page; in the spiritual life, my heart and soul knowledge were very important; in my profession it seemed that only head knowledge was valued. I felt weakened by the divide.

In 2007-8, I spent a year living at Pendle Hill while working as a psychologist in Early Intervention. During that year, I made a commitment to bring more of my heart and soul into my work. I knew the children would be getting a better deal from me if they had all of me, head, heart, and soul along with my body being present. For a year, in an attempt to get more in touch with my heart and soul's responses to the children I saw, when I did a psychological evaluation, while writing a poem or making a painting, I did my best to listen deeply, beyond the intellectual, objective, or clinical demands of my job.

In my study of the spiritual life, I found many researchers and writers who have explored children's spirituality. They defined spirituality inclusively as that part of us which seeks meaning and connection. I found myself needing to explore those things for myself. What I found was that meaning and connection are important to children as well. As I explored further, I found those things are often at least as important to young children as they are to adults. And when the child's need for meaning and connection is addressed, many other areas of functioning fall into place. There are researchers exploring how schools can support this area of children's functioning.

For me, that was exciting! But what were they studying?

Children's spirituality, what is it?

The word spirituality is over-used, but it represents something important. My story about Amy reflects something of what the word means to me and suggests how I want to define "children's spirituality."

I find Spirit way too big to define, but some admirable attempts have been made. To encourage further discourse, the Fetzer Institute struggled and said, "By Spirit we mean the universal spirit that is the deepest and most inclusive ground of being. Spirit is the source of all that exists. Spirit is the infinite, creative energy that gives birth to the universe. Spirit is the common source of the world's faith traditions. Spirit is the love that creates and sustains life."

This definition serves my purpose for talking about children's spirituality.

William Penn wrote about the "word in the heart from which all scriptures come." This deep inner source that takes us beyond ourselves is described in the Gospel of John as the logos or "Word." It's the Spirit with which children so often freely commune. It's the source of wonder that calls a three-year-old girl to see so much more in a flower, a rock, or a piece of bark.

Tobin Hart in his incredible book "The Secret Spiritual World of Children," speaks of children's spiritual moments. Spiritual moments are moments of awe, wonder, being infused with wisdom beyond one's years, asking questions about meaning and life, and seeing the invisible spiritual world of angels and spiritual beings. My moment with Amy was a spiritual moment.

When I speak of children's spirituality, I am not referring to their connection to any particular religion, creed, or doctrine but about a special kind of children's energy. The place of creation energy that connects each of us to that which is bigger than ourselves is perhaps best represented by flowers, feathers or leaves floating on the creek. As children well know, it's not found in hammers of creed or doctrine.

Children are spiritual beings who experience spiritual moments in their lives. As adults we have denied that reality for too long. When acknowledged, this spiritual reality of children can serve as foundational strength for building the cognitive, communicative, adaptive, social/emotional, and physical domains that are now recognized as important for young children.

The concept of narrative prisons is important here. Adults have developed stories about children's spirituality that hold children captive in small boxes; for many children the small boxes holding their souls captive can create pathology. Children then act out as an attempt to break out of the smallness we hold them in and disordered patterns start to develop. Universal, cultural, or societal narrative prisons are taken in by children and become personal narrative prisons. The universal becomes the personal and the personal becomes the universal.

Creating parenting and educational structures that allow the largeness of spirit creates freedom to grow and be in the bigger place in the universe, a place that children know and yearn for. To break out of our narrative prisons, we need to ask questions and discuss the possibilities for answering these hard questions. Acknowledging and nurturing children's spirituality can help them become the persons they were intended to be, and our world will benefit.

In my other life, as a Quaker, I was involved in research related to "out-of-the-ordinary spiritual experiences." I was then involved in a research project related to children's spiritual experiences. I couldn't help but ask myself if a child's behavior would not be drastically affected if they were having out-of-the-ordinary experiences for which they had no vocabulary, understanding, or people to talk to about it (even when words were inadequate). And I had to conclude that the answer was yes. I wanted to know more. I was involved in this line of research for about 12 years. It was amazing! And I believe that work is very compatible with the work psychologists and educators are doing in schools. We have to allow our work with children to go beyond the latest regulations and dictated forms and protocols! Our world is complex. Our children need many tools for surviving and thriving that are not measured on our standardized tests. I do not believe there is good predictive validity between our test items and later success in relating with the myriad of experiences that come our way in this complex world. This complexity necessitates a foundation in spiritual, meaning-making, ethical models, and a connection with ourselves and others that takes more than basic social skills–skills which are critical to success and thriving in our complex world. In the past, churches and faith communities provided some of that kind of training under the rubric of religion. Many children today are getting the foundational grounding in these essential skills nowhere. As educators, we present children a huge informal curriculum that is not done in an intentional manner (for example, in the books we choose to read them at story hour). I believe we must present this informal curriculum in a more intentional way, that begins to address the widening gap that exists between what children are formally taught and what is actually needed for them to adapt to the complexities around them.

From the exploratory research done on children's spirituality, several thoughts came forward for further exploration. These include the following ideas: The normal is narrowed in our culture by giving out diagnoses, quantifying abnormalities as sickness, not merely qualitative differences. Those with diagnoses are stigmatized. Adults determine how large or small a child's universe remains, and most make it too small. Our culture makes norms that exclude spirituality and expects conformity to them. This results in creating difficulties for some people in functioning.

When a child does not fit into a school situation, we need to ask, "What does this child need? Are some of the child's needs spiritual? Does the framework we are using to assess this child open up life or shut it down? What is good about this child's energy? What are this child's gifts? How might they contribute to making the group's experience a richer one?" Some children need the access to mental health services that a diagnosis gives, but might they also be helped by being listened to and respected as spiritual beings. Perhaps they have neurological differences. Often when creativity and special gifts are not framed in a way that allows for those differences to be used as gifts, they can become destructive. This child might be a visionary that the culture especially needs. We might approach educating children not just from the outside in, but by listening to what they are experiencing and connecting our lessons to the feelings and questions raised inside them by their experiences. We might expect that education that evolves this way will involve physical movement and creative chaos as it those experiences are worked through. True science is connected to inner experience.

Cross-Cultural Study (This could be a book in itself. I will just give you a flavor of the experience!)

I spent the summer of 1988 traveling in Asia and visiting schools all over Taiwan, many places in Japan, and in Bangkok, Thailand. I saw many ways in which little children are educated differently and special needs are viewed in many different ways.

In early 2017, I spent five weeks in Qatar, Africa, and Asia. In Doha, Qatar, my niece was teaching at an international school. The children she taught included children from the royal families. Many had nannies who even dressed them. Her relationships with parents were very different from most of ours, much more deference required.

In direct contrast to the wealth of Qatar in the Middle East, I visited a school in Kenya for very young children called "Children of Hope." The children there are called vulnerable children, another word for special needs but they do not have special education as we know it. The school is part of a compound of hand-built houses made of mud bricks, a community in which those who run the school live along with some of the children. They try to address each child's needs and attempt to raise the money to provide each child one meal a day. I created what I call the "Porridge Team" to raise money to make sure each of those little children get their one meal a day. The director, Bonface, sends me emails often telling me how the children learn so much better when they have a meal and are not hungry, along with pictures of activities the children are engaged in. I am grateful for the opportunity to help with an effort such as this, knowing where the money goes and that it is well-spent. Children definitely learn better when they are not physically hungry.

I assert that children also learn better when they are not emotionally or spiritually hungry.

I then visited a school for leadership training for girls in Tanzania. That program was much more structured, strict, and demanding. I witnessed a lot of shaming over wrong-doing and there was a lot of "wrong-doing" of extremely minor infractions (in my biased way of thinking, minor). The girls were very grateful to be there and felt honored to be chosen for an education that would place them in a position of leadership in their communities.

The experience that most stayed with me was a requested visit to a school in Nepal. In Nepal, I was hosted by a friend of a friend, Shamsher. I had been introduced by email and expected him to tell me a nice place to stay and what to see. Instead, he hosted me in his home with his family. For eight days, he showed me Nepal, including trekking in the Himalayas and attending many traditional celebrations to help me get to know the cultural traditions of the Newar people. His brother-in-law ran a school. When they heard that I was a School Psychologist by profession, they asked me to come and help them with a situation with a little girl. I explained that I was not licensed to work in Nepal. They explained that they have no such regulations and they just needed my help. I met with them and the little girl with her sister. I then made some simple recommendations. Not knowing their culture, I did not want to offend in any way, but said what I thought based on a simple consultation. They and the child's parents and teachers expressed great appreciation and still correspond with me from time to time.

Seeing how education and special education are done in other countries gives me appreciation and perspective on our own systems.

Creativity for Everyone

In second grade, I learned that art was for the talented and I was not talented. I did not draw the flower as the teacher expected. In my practice of Arts and Spirituality, I offer that everyone is creative in different ways but that everyone is creative. Some create through writing, visual art, dance, writing great lesson plans; life becomes the medium. I am always especially shocked when parents tell me they are not creative. Creating children is the most important way to be creative. Other creations that are important include building community, learning to solve conflicts, and all ways of relating successfully with fellow human beings. Communication, when it happens, is a miracle of creation.

I have written about my experiences with Arts and Spirituality (Art as Soul's Sanctuary, 2018). Like with this book, in that writing, I use my visual art and writing to express my creativity and perspective on this practice. Focusing on creativity is important in bringing the right-brain balance I believe to be so important to our work as educators. All children need their strengths and uniqueness in creative expression to be affirmed and nourished.

My Flower Dedicated to My 2nd Grade Teacher

(Un-learning Her Lesson and Learning that I Am Creative TOO!)

The Integrative Process

I have worked in a public educational setting that promotes a secular life. Conflicts that create my divided life have ranged from general philosophical struggles to specific struggles regarding action in the present moment. These divided life struggles can arise from organizational structure, dictated by an external source, or they can arise from an internal source, as I struggle to live my own spiritual principles, such as struggles to do what I believe to be in the best interests of the children I serve. Some cases bring forth these struggles from more than one source. Later, I will discuss the case of Willard, one example of how these struggles manifested. I will contrast what was required of me in my employment with what is required of me by my faith.

I would like to say that I will also include a resolution to these struggles and a nice tidy conclusion, but I have no such conclusion to offer.

In fact, I am coming to realize that there may be as much value in the struggle to integrate my life as there may be in that nice tidy conclusion we all seem to seek.

In EI the children are three- to five-years-old. Many people ask me, "How could children so young require the services of a psychologist?" I sometimes respond, "If you knew how many children were being kicked out of preschool, you would be amazed and hopefully appalled.

This book represents a sampling of the results of my experiment with heart-and soul-centered practice, in a setting and profession where my experiment might not be understood. I now view this heart-and soul-centered practice along with strength-based approaches as the hope for the future of our children and for the education systems that are sometimes not equipping them for succeeding in their later lives.

Years of research in child development have identified some of the essential requirements for kids to become happy, successful adults. (Remember Abraham Maslow's Hierarchy of Needs?)

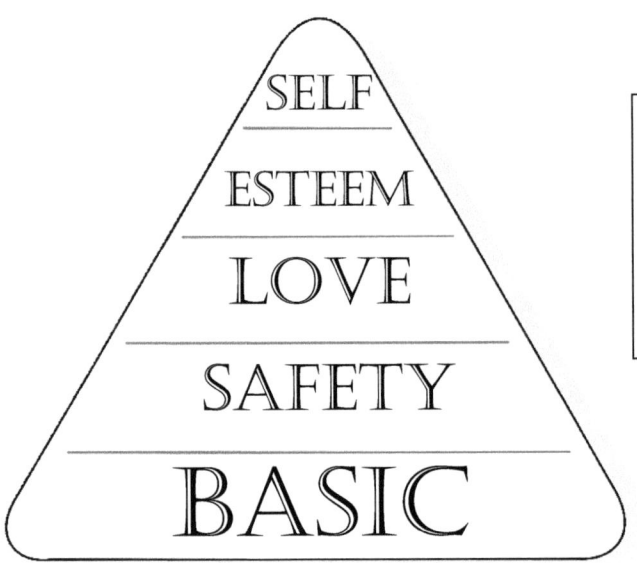

An overly simplified version of Maslow's Hierarchy of Needs. Adults need all levels to be met before the apex of "Self-Actualization" can be achieved.

Children have those needs, too.

I have seen no research in developmental psychology that says kids need to live in fancy mansions, to play with high-tech gadgets or video games, or to wear fancy clothes. I think history will teach us that both extreme poverty and extreme wealth are bad for kids. Yet that is the direction our country seems to be moving in: a greater gap in wealth – more really rich folks and more really poor people.

Why are we doing that?

Here is what your kids need to SUCCEED:

Security:
Kids must feel safe and sound. This means providing them with basic survival needs: shelter, food, clothing, medical care, and protection from harm.

Unconditional Love:
Saying and showing you love your kids can overcome almost any parenting "mistakes" you might make. Even when your kids have disobeyed, angered, frustrated, and rebelled against you, they must know that you love them and that you'll always love them.

Continuity/Consistency:
Parents must synchronize their parenting. No "good cop, bad cop." This also means that important values should not be changed or disregarded casually or for convenience. Consistency can also come from family and community. Ideally, a family remains together in a stable household. But when that ideal breaks down, your child's life must be disrupted as little as possible. Kids and families should also be part of larger units to give them a sense of belonging and cultural continuity.

Constructive role models:
Parents are their kids' first and most important role models.
Be the kind of person you want them to become.

Emotional support:
Parents' words and actions should facilitate kids' trust, respect, self-esteem, and, ultimately, independence.

Education:
Make sure your kids get the best possible education for their future. This includes school, but it also includes the invaluable lessons about life that you provide during the time you spend together. Home is the first school.

Defined Structure:
Rules, boundaries, and limits. Without them, kids are forced to be adults before they are ready, and they lose respect for you and other adults.

11 of the Most Commonly Used Replacement Behaviors

Over the years, I have conducted countless evaluations, and the following are the things I most often find myself recommending to teachers and parents that are important for children to begin learning:

1. PLAY SKILLS for little children are most important! Most of the rest follow from here.
2. Expressing wants, needs, ideas, and feelings (especially labeling feeling words) in effective and acceptable ways
3. Getting the attention one needs in ways that are effective and acceptable
4. Coping skills for anger, frustration and fear such as relaxation skills
5. Healthy Self-Talk
6. Basic Social Skills: greeting others, inviting a peer to play, sustaining volleys of interaction
7. Waiting, handling transition
8. Sharing, turn taking
9. Group skills: waiting, raising hand, answering questions, commenting
10. Empathy: putting oneself in the shoes of another (e.g., guessing what another child is feeling)
11. Conflict Resolution skills

Can young children as young as three start to learn these skills? Even those with disabilities?
My experience says yes.

Are these critical skills to teach to young children?
My experience says yes.

Radical Honesty, Truth-telling, and a Principled Life: Willard

My faith requires of me: radical honesty, truth-telling, and a principled life. My employer required of me: relative pragmatic legalism. Those often conflict. I will share a bit about a case to illustrate.

Recently I did a re-evaluation for Willard, a child in our autism support program. His teacher was concerned because he did not seem to be a child with autism. Since I was the psychologist covering that classroom, I did the re-evaluation. Not imagining that the parent would be unhappy about finding out their child did not have autism, I proceeded in the usual, routine way. Suddenly mid-stream, I learned that the parent had put in a complaint that the autism diagnosis had been removed. Nothing had prepared me for the moment when I saw a mother who was upset to find that her child did not have autism.

Then I discovered that this was not the first complaint the mother had made. In the child's initial evaluation, he was found not to have autism, even though a developmental pediatrician had diagnosed him. But unwilling to fight with a parent, my bosses had determined the best course of action was to give the child the diagnosis as a "mediation concession."

My bosses said they were not going to fight with this mom because it would be very expensive, and we would likely lose. I was not given a choice in the matter. Once again, the child was given the diagnosis of autism as a mediation concession; my supervisor told Willard's mom we would give him back the diagnosis since we were "not sure."

I was radically honest despite the risks; Willard and I lost to pragmatic legalism in education. I pray hard for that child and all the many children I have encountered in recent years whose parents need them to be sicker than they are. This was just one of many kinds of situations where nothing in my experience or training had adequately prepared me. In my initial years as a psychologist, the role of administrators was more supportive of children and psychologists. That is what I had come to expect, but something changed. I began to encounter administrators whose priority was not what was best for children but what was legally pragmatic. This was another situation I was not prepared for by training or experience, one that became the organizational source of many of my divided life struggles.

In my depths, I know that our souls need to be seen and that we need to be heard. Only by listening deeply to the children can we hear their pain. Only by listening deeply can we know that their behavior is about their deepest needs not being met; at this age, it is not usually about defying the adults around them, as many teachers and parents seem to believe. Most children cannot get that far. Most cannot get beyond their deep needs to be seen and heard for the people they are, to be affirmed and loved just as they are, despite the adult's needs to "fix" them, to label them as sick, or to reject or abandon them.

Creativity, Compassion and Connection
Not to replace the academic, intellectual practices -- only to deepen them!

Part I. Assessment and Intervention

Assessment and Intervention planning usually takes several hours, so the evaluator gets to know the child, their family, and their teachers fairly well.

Contents:

Emma: Pediatric Bi-Polar

Jane: Abuse, Divorce, and Living in a Shelter

Thomas: Many Languages

Micha: So Smart and Bored by 4

Malcolm: Words are NOT His First Language

Sten: Screaming in Pain

McKenna: The New Kid

Chip: Authenticity

Jayden: Who Is the Client?

Robin: Meaningless Activities

Carl: Labeled "Violent" at 3

Elsie: Class Warfare

Lyle: Labeled a Problem

John: Must we Label Ones so Young?

Lawrence: Needs a Bigger Box

Starla: Forgive Limitations

Brandon: Not Conforming to Expectations

Ready to Party -- Be Yourself
Dedicated to Emma

Emma
Pediatric Bi-Polar?

At 3, you come to be evaluated for special education in your special party dress
That you bought with your savings from your piggy bank.

You come, ready to have a party with us.
You laugh with us, enjoy us;
We enjoy you too, a lot.
We connect powerfully.
We have a fun party.
We see your spirit as big as the sea and bright as the stars!

So beautiful, so smart, so creative;
You love to sing, dance, draw, paint, act,
and at school
You know the answers to all the teachers' questions,
You have friends,
You know how to succeed in school,
You can even swim.

Yet, your mama wants you fixed.

She says you are moody,
You want things your way,
You get upset a lot,
You love special, new, but ordinary is not OK,

AND

You are just like your father,
Your grandfather,
Your great-grandmother,
You have bi-polar too, she says.

And she wants you fixed.

My Hopes for Emma

Emma, I hope that you will find the square hole so that you don't spend your whole life as a square peg trying to fit into a round hole; the pain is intense when there is no place where you can be YOU, without anyone wanting to FIX you.

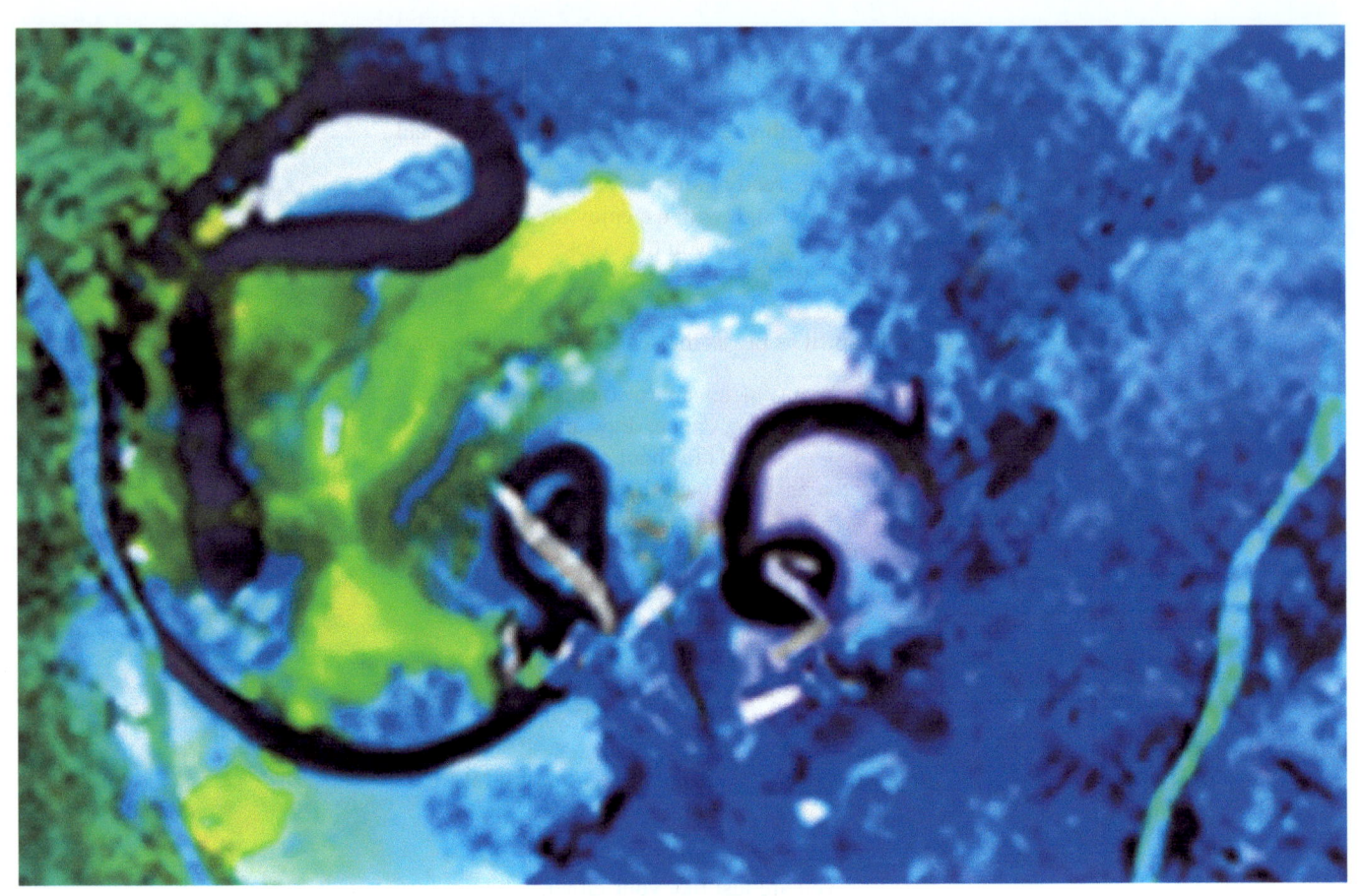

So Beautiful
Drawing Pictures of What Hurts Inside
Dedicated to Jane

Jane
Abuse, Divorce, Living in a Shelter

Your beautiful, free-spirited mama from Jamaica,
Your father from Nairobi,
Met at the Olympics in Atlanta,
Then had you.

But, your daddy thought he wasn't a man
Unless he controlled
The women in his house;
And oh! The results of that!
I am sorry, dear beautiful Jane,
That you have witnessed so much abuse,
And had to leave your home,
Even your state, to be safe.

You are so beautiful and so very smart;
At four years old,
A soul that is old as the hills.

Your mama loves you so much,
But you doubt that love, since your daddy told you she doesn't.

I see you in school, answering the teacher's questions,
Making friends, and doing so well.

Yet, your mama needs help to understand
It is OK, even expected that you are angry, deeply grieving.
Yes, ma'am, children do grieve their losses.

My Hopes for Jane
Jane, I hope your Mama will listen to you and keep loving you so well.
I hope you will draw many pictures of what hurts inside.
I hope your mama gets what she needs so she CAN keep loving you so well!

Words Bursting Forth as the Sun Rises in the Morning
Words Bursting Forth SOON
Dedicated to Thomas

Thomas
Many Languages

Language is the issue they say;
How can I know why words are difficult for you?

Romanian, Russian, and English,
Three words for the same things;
Sometimes too many choices can cripple,
As it seems is the case for you.

Maybe you really can't acquire language,
but how will we know?

Strategies
I hear you needing time to sort it all out,
I hear you needing practice,
I hear you needing models,
I hear you needing coaching,
I hear you needing to be accepted as you are.

My Hopes for Thomas

Thomas, I hope that the fire within you will soon burst forth with

WORDS

Just as the sun rises above the earth every morning.

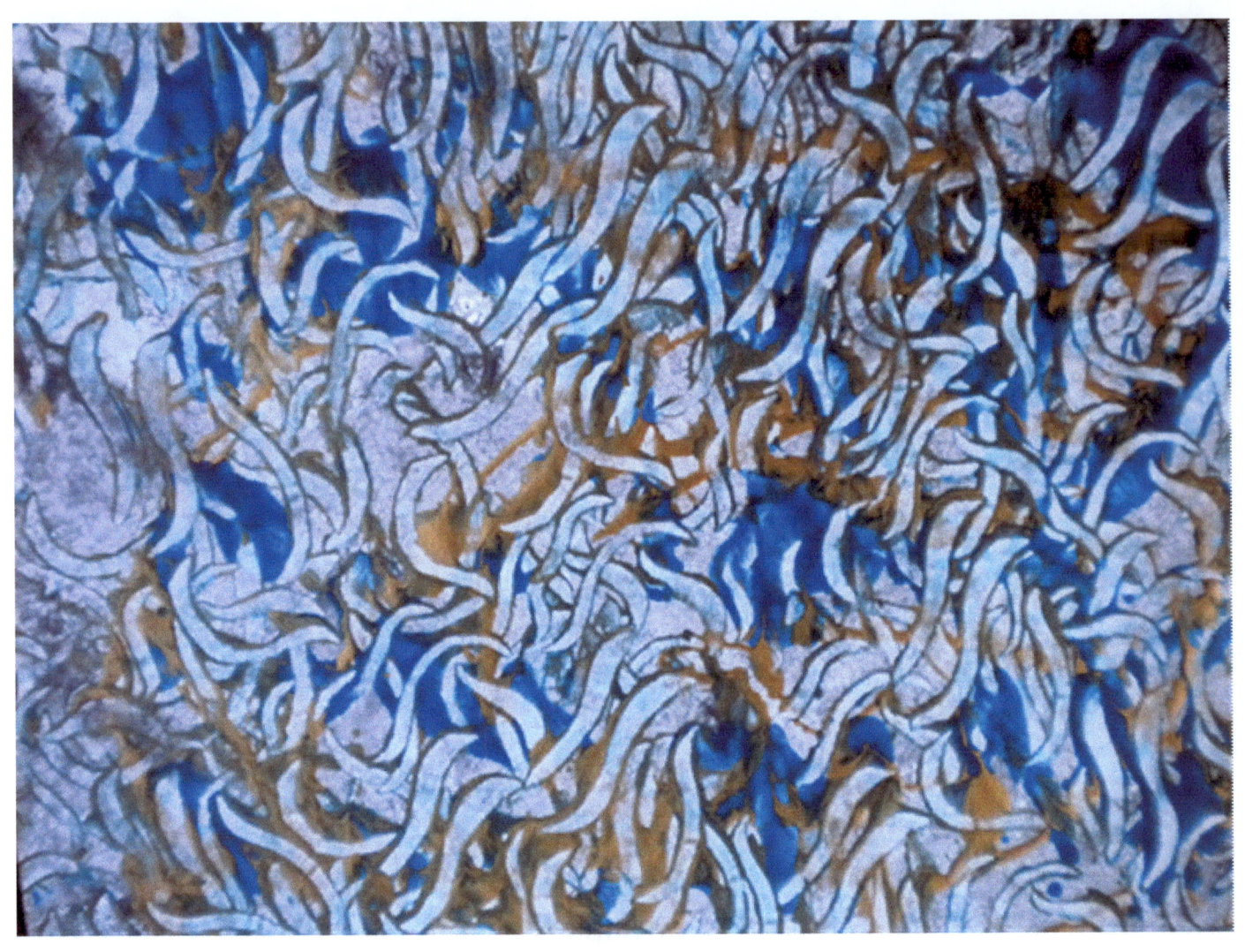

**Loving Learning
Dedicated to Micha**

Micha
So Smart and Bored by 4

Big brown eyes
So verbal
So connected
So loving
So energetic,
ADHD not!

My diagnosis:
Excited about learning
Smarter than your teacher or parents.
So curious.
Hard to challenge, hard to keep from boredom!

A delightful boy
Hard to contain
In the preschool where you are bored,
That asks you to sit still
From 9-5 all day, every day!

I loved playing with you!
I told your mom to tell those worried relatives to
Start saving for college
Because you are going far and your
Mama knows it.

You are so so so loved!

My Hopes for Micha
Micha, may you soon find the place, the teachers who can communicate with you and see you and who you are, even when you do not fit their protocols.
May your love of learning NEVER be squashed!

Beyond the Demand for Words
Dedicated to Malcolm

Malcolm
Words are NOT His First Language

So smart
So creative
So athletic
So gorgeous
So physical
Labeled aggressive, NOT!

I see you expressing yourself physically
Because that is your first language.

The teacher says, "use your words"
A thousand times a day;
But no matter how many times she says it,
Words are still not your first language.

I see you trying to translate so much into words
But the intellect is so keen,
It is hard to translate fast enough.

Maybe you won't be a lawyer like your mom,
Maybe words will never be your first language,
But I'll bet once you get the hang of the
TRANSLATION,
There will be no stopping you.

Yes, I WILL vote for you for president!

My Hopes for Malcolm
Malcolm, may those around you be able to listen deeply and hear you, beyond the demands for words, to see your amazing strengths, to see YOU, to hear YOU.

**May the Pain Be Eased;
Keep Surprising Us with Your Learning
Dedicated to Sten**

Sten
Screams in Pain

As you scream, my heart screams with you!
Where is your pain?
What is your pain?
So intense---

Your attention fleeting,
One thing then the next –
The pain too intense to focus,
You keep moving.

Then, surprise,
Those puzzles, numbers, letters,
You know them!

My Hopes for Sten
Sten, may your pain be lessened. May a way be found to stop your screaming; may your pain stop so that you can be the smart, creative person you are intended to be.
Keep surprising us with how much you know!

Being Where You Want to Be, OUTSIDE
Dedicated to McKenna

McKenna
The New Kid

New kid to school, to this state, actually.
Bib overalls, so cute;
You must fulfill your mother's dream in that way!

You look over at me
But are NOT interested.
As you move from toy to toy,
What are you thinking?

Then it is crystal clear,
You run straight for your book bag,
No doubt –
You want outta here NOW!
We, who seemed not to exist,
Suddenly are let know
You want to go HOME NOW
Or at least outside.

OK, says the teacher,
In five minutes, we go outside;
YEAH, a brief reprieve to the outdoors.

BUT, you must paint the squirrel,
Then you can go outside.
So, your hands paint the squirrel;
Your heart is already outside,
And painting the squirrel seems the last thing you'd
Ever want to do.

My Hopes for McKenna

McKenna, may you find a way to be where you need to be; may you find a way to paint fewer squirrels or find a way to love the things that you are required to do at school. May your teacher find your loves and allow you to be with them, even if they are outside!

Authenticity in Caring and Desires
Dedicated to Chip

Chip
Authenticity

You greeted me, genuinely,
That other child cried; you hugged him, genuinely.

Sometimes it seems urgent
And you whine for a few moments
To get your way, impatient.

But, school is not where you want to be
Or what you want to be doing.

Yet, you comply most of the time.
My heart goes out to you.
I wish we could just go outside and play, right now.

My Hopes for Chip
Chip, thank you for your genuineness and authenticity; you pretend in your play but your heart does not deceive. May you find and engage in what your heart authentically desires and may your authenticity serve as a model for others!

May Your Family Find Your Way in this New Place:
Light and Strength Shine Through
Dedicated to Jayden

Jayden
Who is the client?

Let's see
You are the one being tested;
Your dad says your household is chaos,
Financial disaster.
So, you can't go to school.
And you want to. I am sorry.

Mom's pregnant.
Lost her job.
Oh my….and she is a Beatles fan, you know.
Dad is so stressed,
Looks so tired.
He wants so much for you that he does
not know how to get. I am sorry.

But, why is it, YOU are being tested?
I have not figured that out.

My Hopes for Jayden
Jayden, may your family settle as they move to a new state.
May they love each other well, and find their way through this time of family chaos.
May Jayden's light and strength shine through!

Weaving Our Deepest Selves with the System that Dictates Meaninglessness:
May You Find Your Way
Dedicated to Robin

Robin
Meaningless Activities

A smart guy, they say
Just wants to finish his
Projects, before moving on.

Obviously questioning;
Why must I spend my time on
Meaningless activities?

Put the block under the bear.
Put the block on the bear.
I get it; Robin, you think we are nuts.
We are. Subjecting YOU
To such meaningless activities
Should be criminal.

So polite.
So very polite.
So very very polite.

2-6-year-olds, doing their work;
Line up these blocks
Build a tower
Knock it down
Work this puzzle for the 40th time.

I'm sorry I am testing YOU.
Why am I not testing a system
That requires smart guys like YOU
To sit down and do such
MEANINGLESS activities?

My Hopes for Robin
Robin, may you find your way in a system that requires children to do meaningless activities in the name of testing them. May you find the meaningful work for your life and find the strength to tolerate the meaningless activities of school, along the way. Perhaps rebellion is not always a bad thing; maybe it is a survival tool for some!

May You Be Seen Beyond that Label of "Violent" at Three

Dedicated to Carl

Carl

Violent

Age, just turned 3
I see you screaming, kicking,
Scared to death
of this new place called school.

I see your teachers
Exasperated;
Your report says you are VIOLENT;
they don't know what to do with you.

Your tears, your
snot covers your face.
I get a Kleenex and tell
you I will be gentle…and I am.

Dear little Carl, with
so much power, you have needed to survive.
Foster care, at 3. I feel
the darkness in your life AND
I feel the Spirit.

Almost reaching my knees, your
little arms go up to me.
I hold you tight for a moment and
get my body as still as it can be.
You respond, almost immediately, with
stillness in return.

I walk to the ball pit, carrying you.
I put you down and
jump in. You follow. And
we throw balls at the wall for a
couple of minutes. Intervention not published.
Then you sit with me as
we swing for a two more minutes.
Magic has happened!!

I take your hand. We walk
back to class and I softly
and slowly tell you I KNOW you'll
do a great job in class today and you'll
love school. You say not a word.

You proudly walk in the classroom. You
sit at the table and join in, making letters
In shaving cream.

Ah, I made a new friend today, Carl!
I am happy!!

On Thursday I check in: doing great.
On Friday I check in: doing great.
On Tuesday I check in: doing great.
I can only see your huge potential
when allowed to blossom.

I have so many friends that are called "violent"
3-year-olds. I am glad you are my friends!

Dedicated to Elsie

Elsie
Class Warfare

Your Mama says you have lived in the Princess Suite now for a year;
She does not want to hear about your first life; that is the past;
You should be fixed and fine by now.

Even though, at birth you were abandoned by your birth mother,
Left in the hospital alone with major illnesses for five months,
Separated from your twin.

Then placed in a Russian orphanage where
You were held for half an hour a week and bathed;
But the rest of the time were left with the other ten
babies that you lived with.

From her description of you, I expected to see a monster;
The monster that has destroyed her harmonious wealthy family,
The monster she says has "attachment disorder,"
The monster she says is not allowed to attach to others, if not her,
The monster that is not fixed,
despite having lived in the Princess Suite for a whole year now.
She wants to send you back, she says.

Instead there you are, quite small for 3 ½;
Wearing that purple baseball cap turned backwards,
With those striped pink sunglasses, just trying so very hard
To figure out how to blow those bubbles.
Then it happens; that soapy liquid becomes a bubble,
Just like the other children have; and I see
You want to share it with your new friends.

Then it's snack time. A fudgsicle. It's warm out.
I see you trying so hard to figure out how
To lick that sweet, chocolaty, gooey, delightful stuff,
Without getting it on those precious shorts or shirt.
THAT is a challenge!

You have come so far, I applaud you!

My Hopes for Elsie

Elsie, may your Mama gain patience and compassion, and your teachers too. May they see how hard you are trying; may they see how far you have come and not just how far you have to go to be "fixed" in their eyes, from their judgments of what "fixed" would look like. May you find small places, at least, where you are appreciated and affirmed as the beautiful, delightful child that you are now and are becoming even more of.

Dedicated to Lyle

Lyle

"Hi, I'm Ms. Jen!"
"Hi, I'm Lyle!"

Lyle, a 3-year-old,
Super smart guy.

Active,
Your body needs to MOVE to grow healthy!

Verbal, social, creative.

Yet, another smart, creative, physical boy being labeled a problem –

I am sad for that!

Oh, add Chip to that list too, and Malcolm.

And more and more and more and more.

My Hopes for Lyle

I hope the adults around you recognize and give you the space you need to move and grow,

and that some will even have the energy to move with you!

Maybe then they will see the smart, social, creative boy you are, not a problem.

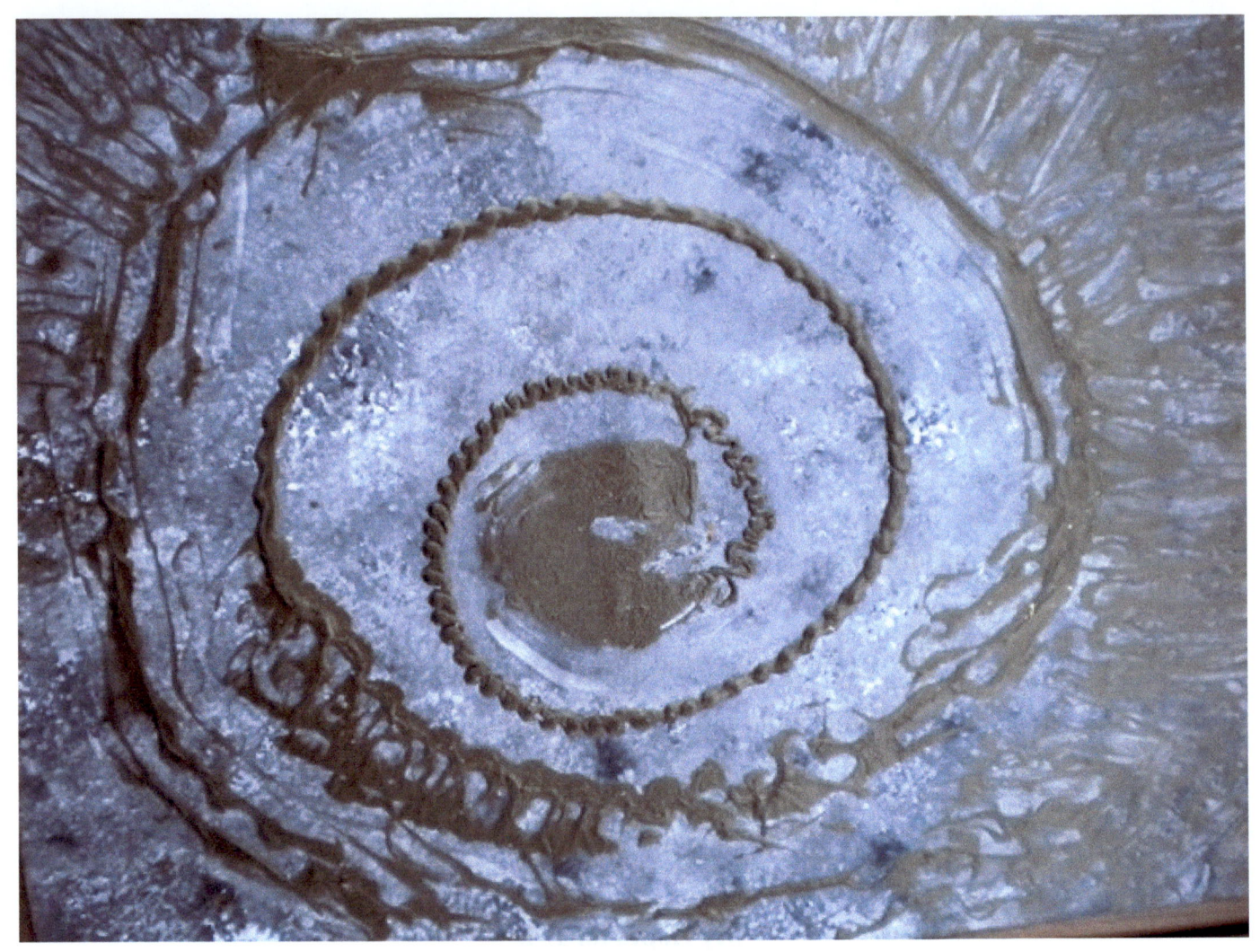

Dedicated to John

John

So young – yet a baby, really.

Having to go to school, function

In groups when you just want to be

And to be held at your mother's breast.

But they love you there; I am so very

Grateful; so young

To feel your parents' conflict, so deep.

Delay does not best fit you; survivor is a better label;

Since I must give you a label.

Your doctor fears autism: wrong.

Smart, you will go far.

Come out of your shell: your task.

To trust those who are not trustworthy –

Not an easy task.

My Hopes for John

I know the shell. Break out of it, for it will not truly protect you.

Dedicated to Lawrence

Lawrence

I hear your need for attention.
I hear your fear.
Your Dad lost his job.
Your Mommy hurt her back.
Your class changed, not play anymore.
Lots of changes. And you are growing.

They wonder why your behavior has changed.

You are smart.
You imitate.
You use humor.
You love music.
You love other kids.
You were diagnosed as autistic.

Diagnosed autistic and NOT, or maybe we cured you.

Lawrence processes what you say by saying it back.

So say Lawrence is smart.

He is Smart.

He can pay attention.

He will hear you and say back what you say.

My Hopes for Lawrence

Parents and teachers, please please open up the small box you have put Lawrence in. Give him room to be the delightful child that he is. Parents please say ok. Parents please say goodbye to us.

(And then, Dad says it, "OK. Let's go get the beast."…Well at least he said OK)

Dedicated to Starla

Starla

Starla! What a perfect name!
Your Beauty radiates; let your lives radiate,
Says the ministry yesterday.

Those eye-catching pigtails;
Your plack eyes pierce my heart.

As you pointedly as why repeatedly,
I wish I knew why.

Why did your mom need drugs when pregant with you?
Why do you have to wear a shunt under that beautiful black hair?
Why does your father say he is coming, and then not come?
Why does your family who loves you so much, EXPECT problems?
Why don't they understand that you are not being defiant, only doing the best you can?
Why is there no compassion left for you?
Why no understanding that you get overwhelmed?
Why no forgiveness for your limitations?

So much to deal with.
So much to deal with at 3.

You attached to me
For a beautiful moment;
We wrote a book together.

I loved that moment; so did you.
Thank you for sharing a moment with me!

My Hopes for Starla

I hope for the wisdom to work with Starla's Aunt. I hope Starla will find what she needs to grow strong and reach her highest potential. May she develop a new healthy brain.

Dedicated to Brandon

Brandon

The architect,
So sensitive,
And you don't know your letters.

You love misic,
and you are so frustrated.
I hear you loud and clear.

Crying to be seen.
Crying to be heard.
See me for who I am, you cry.
See what is sooo right with me, you cry.

The forest lost for the trees.
Match me with a teacher who can see me, please.

I am not like my twin.
I am ME.
I am NOT bad.
I am NOT defective.

See, I love to build things.
See, I love music.
See, I think so deeply.
See, I can love so deeply.
See, I am hurting so badly.

I cannot conform to your demands;
please stop comparing me.
Please. Please. Please.

Mom and Dad so frustrated,
Mom and Dad so concerned.
Mom and Dad so seduced by expectations
of conformity.

I will learn my letters, not just yet.
I will learn to socialize, not just yet.

Out-of-sync you call me;
But, really, I am in-sync with my spirit.
The world needs my sensitivities.

I AM in-sync!

My Hopes for Brandon
I hope your creations will someday be seen, and your music someday heard. I see you. I hear you.
I hope the rest of the world will get that opportunity, and
I hope that time comes soon, for all our sakes!

Part II. Consultation

Consultation usually involves only observing the child and interviewing the parents and teachers. This is a less-involved process and the evaluator gets to know the child, but less well than in a full evaluation.

Contents:

Summer: Your Name Fits You So Well

Andy: Who Do YOU love?

Connie: Angels and Fairies

Kyle: Learning to Socialize

Romeo: Focusing that Energy

Elsie: Doing SO Well, But Not FIXED Yet

Jewel: Not Autistic…Just Never Learned English, Yet

Kris: Rock Star

Dena: Just Go Outside

Marco: Family Held Hostage

Bebe: Climbing the Walls, Literally, Until…

Aram: Contemplative

Cole: 12 Psychotropic Meds, Really?

Your Name Fits You So Well
Dedicated to Summer

Summer,
Your Mom used drugs and now you pay the price with learning difficulties. I see you trying so hard, wanting so badly to do it "right" to please the adults. I love your name; it fits you so well.

Who Do YOU Love?
Dedicated to Andy

Andy,
You come to us having been violently physically abused.
Yet, the love you exudeis so authentic and freely given to EVERYONE.
Your openness and your ability to ask all of us,"Who do YOU love?" has touched me deeply.

**Angels and Fairies
Dedicated to Connie**

Connie,
You see the angels and dance with the fairies…I love that! But, at school, you have to learn to be careful who you talk to about that. I want you to know that there are many others who also talk with the angels, but you may not find them in school. Keep looking until you find safety in sharing and you find others who would love to talk to the angels with you!

Learning to Socialize
Dedicated to Kyle

Kyle,
Your Mom has been surfin' the web and has four diagnoses she insists that I give you. You have just turned three and you just don't get it yet how to socialize with other kids, but you are trying. I saw you go up to Alissa and try to hug her and ask her to play. I saw you approach Bobby and put your arm on his shoulder to comfort him when he fell down. I KNOW you are going to be OK.

Focusing that Energy
Dedicated to Romeo

Romeo,
You have so much energy; your teachers cannot keep up with you. You are so often "in trouble." I wish we could bottle that energy; we'd get rich! You are so smart. I can envision you focusing that energy, becoming a successful adult who loves and mentors children, and teaching them to succeed, like you.

Doing So Well, But Not Fixed YET
Dedicated to Elsie

Elsie,
...came from another country…a twin, separated…abandoned at birth…orphanage, held once a week...
Now 3, pretty good English, being careful not to get that ice cream on your
pretty purple dress, and those matching purple sunglasses got MY attention…yet,
Mom wants to know why you are not FIXED yet. Maybe "fixed" is not the right goal for you.

Not Autistic… Just Never Learned English
Dedicated to Jewel

Jewel,
Nonverbal, aggressive, autistic, delayed…you came from another school and that is what I read in those papers about you. Our teacher took you to the play room. I came to watch and get to know you. Suddenly, CURSE WORDS…not, nonverbal. And do I detect an accent in those curse words? You have never learned English…

Rock Star
Dedicated to Kris

Kris,

So shy and small, not yet 3, delayed they fear. Screaming…but LOVE to dance, sing, drum and play the guitar then the shyness is gone. I envision you on the stage, a star, still playing that guitar and singing your heart out, with your Mom in the audience cheering you on.

Let's Just Go Outside
Dedicated to Dena

Dena
They lock the doors and watch you closely…you will "ESCAPE." I see you just want to be outside.
I see you loving the trees, the grass, the sunshine, and even the rain.
You just want to be in NATURE, not in school.

Family Held Hostage
Dedicated to Marco

Marco,
I got to your house and your family has little furniture and few belongings: they cannot have many things and what they have is locked up. You cannot talk to them, so you destroy things. Autism we call it! Then, I walk in your classroom and see you sitting, listening to the teacher, and signing answers to the questions. When you learned sign language, the world opened up for you! You have come so far and will go so much further. The sun is peeking out and the blue sky is coming through the clouds.
Your family is no longer held hostage by their 3-year-old. Yet, another miracle!

Climbing the Walls, Literally, Until…
Dedicated to Bebe

Bebe,

You HAVE TO move: climb the bookshelves, stand in the window sills, and cannot talk to or connect with us. Again, Autism, we call it. Then one day, I see this little girl walking down the hall, pulling a wagon with a friend in it – and it is YOU, smiling. Another miracle, I call it! And hard work, the teachers call it, rightly! My heart soars with I see you playing with your new FRIENDS.

**Contemplative
Dedicated to Aram**

Aram,
In your own world...autism? Or maybe you are called to the contemplative life of an introvert. What is your world like? Maybe it feels better than being in school.

May I share your world, just for a moment?

**12 Psychotropic Meds, Really?
Dedicated to Cole**

Cole,

Your Mother shows me the bag of 12 medications prescribed by your doctor for your behavior.
I shiver. I watch you become more and more psychotic as your small body rebels.
I beg her to get a second opinion…let's try a different path….

Part III

Life Lessons I Learned at a Young Age that have Served Me Well (Not that I Live Them Perfectly Nor Do You Have to Live them Perfectly to Live Them Well):

And Some that Have Had to be Tweaked Along the Way:

Tell the Truth
Honor your parents (and they don't have to know *everything* you do as an adult)
Listen to your teachers (and discern)
Listen to one another; develop good skills for listening *below the surface*
Think about (discern) what is good for you
Work hard (and don't become a workaholic so that it takes over your life)
Try new things
Keep your promises/ Walk your talk/ Make commitments and keep them
Do your best
Say please and thank you
Be thankful (many times a day)
Remember you are loved
Laugh a lot; humor is important
Accept others who are different from you/ Find the compassionate place in your heart and live there
Look for the good in yourself and others
Be kind and learn what that really means
Pay attention to what you are doing
Pay attention to what is happening (don't put your head in the sand when things go wrong; stand up)
The world is big; explore it; Enjoy what Mother Nature has given us
When you are afraid, say so; be careful who you say it to
Share your life and connect with others
Keep all of life in BALANCE
Say your prayers (and know that means something different for different people)
Listen and Follow your deepest knowings (in what you do with your life, big and small decisions)
Take care of yourself and serve that which is bigger than yourself
Do not waste; waste makes want. My waste means someone else does not get what they need
Taking more than I need is greed. Greed means someone else does not get what they need
Work through hate; don't ignore it but work through it so that it does not stay in your system
"Anything worth doing is worth doing well" doesn't mean perfectly
(desire for excellence is not perfectionism; perfectionism stifles real life)
Live the life you have in a REAL way; observing it and pretending lead to a feeling of not having lived

Be sure all of these have ever-changing meaning and are more than mere words and clichés in your life.

Appendix I
What is Strength-Based Practice?

What I say about it:

Strengths-based approaches concentrate on the inherent strengths of individuals, families, groups and organizations, deploying personal strengths to aid recovery and empowerment.

When the practice is strength-based, we do not ignore problems, but we don't focus solely there either. This may be likened to the more effective medical practice of building the immune system while treating the disease.

Strength-based assessment, intervention, and consultation ask questions like:

- What do we need to do for this child to build a stronger foundation for them to stand on in order to function in the world?
- What are his/her strengths? How can we build on them?
- How can we build resilience?
- How can we help THIS child succeed in the world in which she/he finds him/herself?
- How can we use these strengths to address the child's needs?
- How do we not lose the forest for the trees?

What pediatricians say about it:

"…the strength-based approach gives a broad perspective on development more so than the traditional deficit approach. While the more traditional deficit approach focuses on problems, the asset model encourages health promoting interactions. It specifies what families should be implementing or saying "yes" to for a healthier life."[1]

What mental health professionals say about it:

"Strengths-based practice involves a shift from a deficit approach, which emphasizes problems and pathology, to a positive partnership with the family."[2]

"It is often challenging for mental health practices to move from a pathology-based model to an individualized, strengths-based approach. Practitioners have been socialized to derive at a diagnosis by means of their education and training. The common perception is that an accurate diagnosis helps practitioners to institute the appropriate medical treatment to the consumers. Practitioners are often comfortable and confident in their role as expert. Strengths-based approach requires that practitioners acknowledge that they may not be all significant in the life of consumers. However, practitioners can use their knowledge to help consumers to utilize their strengths and integrate these into the recovery process."[3]

What educators say about it:

"All children bring unique strengths to school, but they learn to think about themselves in ways that align with how adults talk about them. If children in special education become accustomed to thinking of themselves in terms of their learning disabilities, they become fixed on the idea that they will forever be perceived as "deficient." If this is the case, then the best that child will ever do, even given all of the available special education interventions, is reach the minimum expectations."[4]

"A strengths-based educational approach is best understood as a philosophical stance and daily practice that shapes how an individual engages the teaching and learning process."[5]

"**When we educate in a strengths-based fashion, we are not ignoring weakness. Instead, we are reframing weakness into an opportunity for growth.** How that opportunity is organized and shaped has a lot to do with what the student's strengths are. In a strengths-based classroom, we offer the student a chance to learn what they need in the way that they want."[6]

Example of a Strength-Based Approach in the Classroom

Ms. Jane's Class:

I had just read in the news about the opening of an ancient Egyptian tomb estimated to be 4300 years old, and was reminded of a time I was assigned to Ms. Jane's school for two years. Her class met in the basement of the Lutheran church; basements of churches were the locations for many of the preschool classes I visited during the 13 years I was a psychologist for the preschools in my county. I absolutely loved visiting this class and there were many reasons that it was my favorite class to visit. The children were always talking and learning and very excited about learning. I came to observe Lou. Lou had Autism. And Lou could not stop talking about relics from Egyptian history. I thought of Lou and Ms. Jane immediately when I saw this news item. Before meeting Lou, I might not have paid attention but knowing Lou taught me to appreciate Egyptian relics. Many teachers would have tried to make Lou stop talking about this obsession. But, Ms. Jane took a different tack. She let him talk about his passion and she let him get the whole class excited about Egyptian relics. They used this theme to learn math/counting, writing, science, English, spelling – really all academic content areas could be taught using this theme. The young children loved it and they learned spectacularly, and Lou with Autism was NEVER stigmatized. He was a hero to the class and they saw him as very smart and never as weird in any way. Ms. Jane was my hero in the world of education and quite beautifully exemplified how a teacher can implement a strength-based approach to education and treat a child as a respected human being first and foremost.

She did not ignore Lou's problems. She did not ignore any of her students' problems. Because she just did not define Lou by his Autism, Lou and his class thrived beautifully!

Epilogue

And here is probably the most important role that I have discovered as a retired school psychologist. I'll start with a story. My grandfather, McKinley Elam (but we called him FiFi – with long i's), served in World War I, combat in France. In 1919, when he returned to his home in Morgan County, KY, legend has it that there was a war going on related to whether there would be public education. A powerful group said, "NO." My grandfather said, "YES." He started a school. One day, a group ambushed him and intended to beat him up to get rid of the school. But since he had just returned home from combat, he was in top-notch physical condition and beat them up. He declared himself the teacher until it got established and the school remained. I am not an advocate of beating up on each other. I am an advocate for public education. These days, the way to advocate is political. We have taken our public education for granted for a few generations now. But, we are at risk of losing the gains we have made. As educators, we MUST advocate for public education! That is probably our most important activity as educators in these days and times.

What kind of world do we want to live in? The cultural norms for looking out for number 1 (at the expense of others and even using meanness) seems to be increasing. Ethics and morality seem to be considered less often. A few days ago, I happened upon a group of children that looked to be about 9-years-old beating up on one another on the sidewalk and one little guy seemed to be getting a very bad end of the deal. I knew that by the time I figured out who to call, it would be too late. All I could do was witness from my car. I stopped and let them know I was watching. They got very angry at me and called me bad names but the physical violence stopped. I left the scene very sad realizing that these scenes are common for many people. What can I do for individuals? What can I do for education? What can I do within my culture? What am I doing? Why am I doing that? Where are my efforts best spent to get the world I most want?

These are questions I think about a lot in my "retirement."

About the Author and Artist

Jennifer Elam is a licensed Psychologist who studied, taught, researched and practiced Psychology from 1969 until 2014. Before becoming a Psychologist, she studied Sociology/Criminology and has found that perspective unique among psychologists. Looking at the institutions and culture that surround individuals is very helpful in assessing their functioning. She served as a Psychologist for over 30 years teaching at the university level, working in residential treatment, and as a School Psychologist with students aged preschool through adulthood. Her Ph.D. focused on working in Early Intervention (EI), with a dissertation focused on working effectively on EI teams. She retired in 2014.

During graduate school, she was fortunate to have been introduced to a Strength-based practice for working with young children. In addition, she was involved in an extensive research project studying Children's Spirituality through the American Center for the Integration of Spiritually Transformative Experiences. Throughout her life, she has had a travel bug and has enjoyed visiting schools in many countries, gaining a cross-cultural perspective. Her desire has been to find ways to integrate the best of her excellent academic training, research, travel, and spirituality/creativity with her many years of experience with children of all ages, but especially very young children. This book experiments with that integration.

Over the past five years, Jennifer has cared for her parents; both of her parents died in January, 2018. "What comes next after estates settlement?", she wonders. She is working with an Advocacy Team through the Friends Committee on National Legislation, a non-partisan group working on many political issues; the dividedness in her country is a great concern. She is also finding herself drawn to more exploration of her heritage, especially as a person from KY. Reading the book, Hillbilly Elegy, has propelled her on a path to explore her own story of leaving and coming back to Appalachia so many times.

I want to say a large Thank YOU to the thousands of children and families that I have been blessed to interact with over the 30+ years of being a psychologist.

I believe the balance has not been quite right between the left and right brain activities in our work with children, especially young children.

May we right that balance and bring to soul to our work, especially with preschoolers in a new way.
May the children be seen in their strength and potential and may we forever give up focusing
on what they do "wrong", categorizing/labeling them.
May we listen, help them solve their problems, and remind them constantly
of their strength, resilience, value and beauty.
May we begin each new day in gratitude for the blessings we have in our children!

As a psychologist retired due to health problems, I think over my career and wonder what I would like to pass on to those coming after me. My career was rich and unconventional. Might I have something to offer? I hope so. At the heart of all is a hope that we will follow our many rules and regulations and we will do our jobs to help children and family solve problems AND I want us to never forget that those we serve are people first.

May we honor them and always treat them with respect.
May we put their strengths and needs before our mandated protocols and never define children by the pathology; may we see children through their strengths and the gifts they bring to this earth,
while helping them to solve the problems they face.
May we always use our intellectual and academic knowledge for the highest good,
and balance that with heart and soul.

Cited Sources:

1. Strength-Based-Approach. (2018).
   Retrieved from https://www.aap.org/en-us/advocacy-and-policy/aap-health-initiatives/HALF-Implementation-Guide/communicating-with-families/pages/Strength-Based-Approach.aspx.

2. An Individualized, Strengths-Based Approach in Public Child Welfare Driven Systems of Care. (2014).
   Retrieved from https://www.childwelfare.gov/pubs/acloserlook/strengthsbased/strengthsbased1/

3. Xie, H. (2013). Strengths-Based Approach for Mental Health Recovery.
   Retrieved from https://www.ncbi.nlm.nih.gov/pmc/articles/PMC3939995/

4. deBros, Kathryn (2015). Strengths-Based Approach to Teaching Gives Special Education Students Hope.
   Retrieved from https://www.noodle.com/articles/strengths-based-approach-to-teaching-gives-special-education-students-hope191

5. Lopez, Shane J & Louis, Michelle C (2009) The Principles of Strengths-Based Education.
   Retrieved from https://www.tandfonline.com/doi/pdf/10.2202/1940-1639.1041?

6. Rivera, Jade (2018) The Truth About Strengths-Based Education.
   Retrieved from http://www.jadeannrivera.com/strengths-based-education/

Soul Returns to Preschool and other titles by the author are available for purchase on Amazon.com.

For bulk orders, or to schedule a workshop for your group, please contact the author through her website:

http://jenelam.com/

Printed by Libri Plureos GmbH in Hamburg, Germany